Prolance
www.prolancewriting.com
California, USA
© 2020 Heba Subeh-Hyder

ISBN: 978-1-7358468-6-6

Maymunah's Musings

What DID ALLAH create for ME?

Written by:
Heba Subeh-Hyder

Illustrated by:
Aatena Hasan

May Allah
accept my
efforts and
intention.

Bismillah.

I dedicate this book to my Creator, the Most
Beautiful, the Best Artist, Who created everything for
us with beauty and purpose.

I also dedicate this story to my brother and
sister-in-law, for they were the true inspiration behind
Cousins' Week. Without them, the idea for this book
would not have been conceived. Jazakum Allah khair
for all the fun memories you've created for our
children.

--With Love,
Heba

It was the first day of summer break. The sun was bright, and the birds sang their sweet summer songs. A warm, gentle breeze tickled Maymunah's cheeks as she thought of the exciting week to come.

In the Ali household, summer vacation meant one thing and one thing only: Cousins' Week!

Every summer, Maymunah and her brother Malik visited their uncle's family for an entire week full of fun.

Uncle Zayn and Auntie Jamila took the children hiking, fishing, and camping near the lake by their house.

Maymunah's favorite part of Cousins' Week was nighttime, when everyone sat around the campfire and told stories. Auntie Jamila had the best stories, and Uncle Zayn came up with new funny songs each year.

Malik was usually as happy as Maymunah about Cousins' Week, but this year was different. Every time she brought it up to him, he shrugged.

"Why can't I skip it this year?" Malik asked Baba, "I'm too old for it." "You're never too old for cousins' week. You're going to have loads of fun insha'Allah," Baba said.

Maymunah wrinkled her brows. She knew why Malik wanted to stay home.

He wanted to play those annoying video games.

Maymunah didn't know how he could think video games were better than Cousins' Week!

That night, Maymunah barely slept a wink. And the next morning, she sprung right out of bed, even before her alarm went off.

It was finally here!

HONK! HONK!
"Are you sure I can't stay home?" Malik moaned.
"Off you go, Malik," said Mama and Baba.

honk!
honk!

Maymunah dashed out to Uncle Zayn's car with a huge smile on her face, but Malik plodded behind with his head down.

When they finally arrived at the beautiful campsite, their cousins Luna and Deen rushed out of their tents.

"IT'S COUSINS' WEEK!" They shouted, as they wrapped one another in hugs and Deen received his usual head noogie from Malik.

The first activity was hiking. Hikes were done early in the morning, when it was not too hot and not too cold.

While walking the trail, Maymunah looked up at the tall trees that smelled of pine. She ate from blackberry bushes and admired a glistening stream that was so clear you could see the rocks and fish at the bottom. Maymunah even saw some yellow jackets buzzing around but made sure to keep away.

"Look at this big green praying mantis," Luna said, picking it up. She held it close to little Deen, who covered his face.

"GET THAT BUG OUT OF MY FACE!"

"Deen, it might look a bit creepy, but don't worry. It won't hurt you. Remember, Allah created this, too, and everything He made is for us to benefit from," Luna explained.

Deen grimaced. "Even ugly bugs?"

"Yes, even ugly bugs, Deen."

Everyone laughed except for Malik.

Maymunah frowned. She really wished her brother would enjoy the hike. How could he not appreciate all the wonderful things they were seeing?

Suddenly, they heard a scream!

Deen hid behind a tree as a strange looking bird approached him. The bird looked like a mix of a turkey and an eagle.

Deen's eyes were wide and filled with tears.

Malik crept towards Deen. "Don't be afraid. This is a turkey vulture. It's perfectly harmless."

"Are you sure it won't hurt me?" Deen asked, his voice shaking.

"Yes, I learned about these birds in school," Malik said, pulling Deen close and hugging him. "They don't hurt little humans like you."

The bird turned its small red head over its brownish-black feathered body. Then, it flapped its great, big wings and leapt into the sky.

"Cool!" Deen shouted, and they all watched in amazement as it flew away.

Even Malik had a smile on his face.

And after, during fishing, Malik's smile only widened when
Maymunah caught her very first fish: a big, colorful rainbow trout!

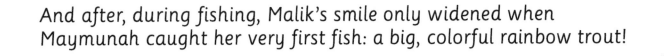

BARAKAH

The sun was setting as everyone made their way back.
They made wudu and prayed Maghrib together.

Afterward, they sat around the crackling fire. Maymunah admired the beautiful sunset. It was purple and blue with some shades of pink mixed in.

Malik sat next to Maymunah and put his arm around her. "I have to say, Cousins' Week turned out better than I thought. I'm sorry if I was such a fun sponge."

Maymunah giggled. Fun sponge was what she and Malik called each other if one of them was being moody.

"I guess I just forgot about all the awesomeness here. I mean, that turkey vulture was pretty cool, wasn't it?"

"Yes, it was. And so was my huge trout!" Maymunah laughed.

Just then, Uncle Zayn started to sing a silly song and the two quieted down to listen.

"Heeeey, hey! It's Cousins' Week! Gonna eat and play, and have fun all daaaay!"

Everyone sang along, each adding their own funny line. Luna played her tablah, and Deen broke out into some serious dance moves.

They were having a great time. Especially Malik.

As the night came to an end, Maymunah crawled into her tent and grabbed Patches, her stuffed cat.

She was grateful to Allah for all the wonderful creation she had seen today: the bugs, the trees, the clear stream, the multicolored rainbow trout, and the gorgeous sunset at Maghrib time. But the creation she was most thankful for was her brother Malik. She felt special to know that Allah made him her brother, and so happy that he was finally enjoying Cousins' Week.

Maymunah read her bedtime surahs and drifted off to sleep with a smile on her face, dreaming of the surprises the rest of this week would bring.

"He Who created all things in the best way and He began the creation of man from clay."
(Quran 32:7)

Activity Time!

Salam, kids! Here's a special activity for you. This story is about Allah's beautiful creation. Can you draw and label all the creation you read about in the space below?

↳ What did you find in the book? ↲

Next, go outside with a grown-up and find three things that Allah created just for you! They could be things you think are beautiful, things you can eat, or things you can play with. After you've found them, draw them below.
Ready? Bismillah, let's go!

What did you find outside? Draw and label!

1.
_____

2.
_____

3.
_____

Glossary

🍃 Allah: Arabic word for God

🍃 Insha'Allah: if God wills

🍃 Barakah: blessing

🍃 Wudu: the cleansing or ablution that Muslims make before performing their prayers

🍃 Maghrib: the prayer performed by Muslims at sunset

🍃 Tablah: drum

🍃 Surahs: chapters/verses from the Quran, the Holy book for Muslims

About the Author:
Heba Subeh-Hyder is a resident of Southern California and a wife to a loving husband, and mother of three wonderful girls.

She has a Bachelor's degree in Management and Human Resources from Cal Poly Pomona, where she was actively involved in the Muslim Student Association, and is currently working on another degree in Islamic Studies from California Islamic University.

Heba has worked as an Executive Team Leader, Office Manager, led a few Islamic halaqas (study circles), and has spoken on panels aimed towards educating the public regarding different topics on Islam.

Her passion for the deen is what inspired her to be an author. Her aim is to nurture our youth's innate belief and love of Allah at a young age, and to encourage reflection by taking them on adventures to discover Allah, subhanahu wa ta'ala through His attributes.

About the Illustrator:
Aatena holds a Computer Science degree. As a hobby, she has done digital art for many years, and has recently delved into traditional painting, specifically using acrylic paint. She loves gaming, visiting new places, trying new kinds of food, and spending time with her cats.